Wanting to be *Born*

THE CRY OF THE SOUL

Wanting to be Born

THE CRY OF THE SOUL

COMPILED BY

Dr. Neroli Duffy M.B.B.S., B.Med.Sci.
Based on the teachings of Elizabeth Clare Prophet

THE SUMMIT LIGHTHOUSE LIBRARY™

WANTING TO BE BORN
The Cry of the Soul
Compiled by Dr. Neroli Duffy
Based on the teachings of Elizabeth Clare Prophet
Copyright © 2002 The Summit Lighthouse Library
All rights reserved.

For information, please contact The Summit Lighthouse Library, PO Box 5000, Corwin Springs, MT 59030-5000, USA.
Tel: 1-800-245-5445 or 406-848-9500.
E-mail: tslinfo@tsl.org
Web site: www.tsl.org

THE SUMMIT LIGHTHOUSE LIBRARY™

Library of Congress Control Number: 2002106149
ISBN: 0-9720402-2-6

Cover art, design and production: Brad Davis
Illustration on page 3: Ilana Myers-Pollyea

Printed in the United States of America

06   05   04   03   02   5   4   3   2   1

To souls of great light,
waiting to be born...

Contents

CONTENTS

Preface

A spiritual understanding of the life of the
soul and her* relationship to the body
being prepared for her has changed the way
that many think about abortion. We offer
these spiritual teachings to enable people
everywhere to make enlightened choices.

Abortion is a complex issue. There are
many arguments for and against it and many
myths. From a spiritual perspective, however,
the answers may be simpler than we think and
more far-reaching than we could ever imagine.

---

*We use the pronouns she and her to refer to the soul because
each soul, whether clothed in a male or female body, is the
feminine aspect of the masculine Spirit, or Higher Self.

A Timetable for Each Soul

*E*very soul has a timetable. Archangels and cosmic beings of light direct the timetables of conception and birth for every child. These timetables are also directed by specific masterful beings who are the sponsors of that soul—the Godparents, if you will. The timetables are part of God's grand design of life.

Think of how wondrously you were made, how God cared for you personally and carefully oversaw your nurturing in the womb. Your Father-Mother God ordained your conception, your parents, your life, your purpose, your reason for being. You were born at the precise moment ordained for you.

What would you do if you had not been born? How would you work out your spiritual destiny?

The abortion of a soul is more than the abortion of the physical body. It is the abortion of that soul's destiny and divine plan. It is the abortion of an individual calling from God, for God chooses the very special moment in history for each soul to return to earth to take part in the divine plan of the decades and the centuries.

When we abort life in the womb, we abort the opportunity of a soul whose timetable for incarnation on earth has come up in the cycles of life.

Even before a child is conceived in the womb, the divine plan of the soul has been worked out in intricate detail. The grand design of God is so exact that, at the moment of conception, the genes in the tiny embryo are already suited to the specific soul who will inhabit it.

Everyone has a mission. Those who undergo a near-death experience often report being told of their mission at meetings with angels and masters of light. These are often called "life reviews." In fact, at the conclusion of their time on earth, each soul takes stock of the life they have lived. The successes and failures are all seen as learning experiences. Those who have returned from a near-death experience often do so because they had a specific mission they had not yet fulfilled. They return with a real sense of purpose, seeking to fulfill what they came to earth to do.

A child enters the womb with a unique mission and the same sense of purpose. Before conception ever takes place, a board of spiritual overseers, together with the Higher Self of the soul, determines when and where and under what circumstances the soul will embody. These circumstances are tailored to the soul's needs in order to give her the best opportunity to work out the purposes of life on earth as well as the specific karma allotted for balancing and clearance in a particular embodiment.

Karma and Reincarnation

The principles of karma and reincarnation can help us understand many of life's challenges. With a deeper understanding of our own place in the universe, we develop a new understanding of the issue of abortion.

Karma is the law of cause and effect—as we sow, so shall we reap. Our thoughts, feelings, words and actions send ripples out into the world. We affect the world even as the world affects us. All of life is energy, and energy is neither created nor destroyed. What we send out to others returns to us after gathering more of its kind.

If we send out positive thoughts, feelings,

actions and words, the same returns to us. If we engage in unkind or harmful behavior, that negative energy cycles back to us for balancing. It can create a debt we owe to the individual who was on the receiving end of our misqualified energy. If we are smart, we will ask for forgiveness and right the wrong that was done. But if the harmful action is not balanced by loving deeds and service to life, we may owe the person or life itself a karmic debt that may come due for payment in a future life.

We make good karma by serving others; by sending out love, peace and compassion; by taking a stand for truth and defending life and right action. We make negative karma by negative actions, words, deeds, thoughts and feelings—as well as by sins of omission and inaction. Not speaking out when we should and sitting back and being an observer when we are supposed to take action are karma-creating decisions.

Life is not a spectator sport. We reap what

we have sown—yesterday, five minutes ago and ten thousand years ago. Interestingly, we do not always reap what we have sown right away. God has ordained the cycles and laws of his universe, and many of us do not reap in a given lifetime what we have sown in that life. But at the right time, as cycles turn, the energy we have sent out will come full circle.

The end of an age and the beginning of a new one (from the age of Pisces to the dawning age of Aquarius) is a time for many things to return for resolution. Karma returns to our doorstep to be balanced. The more we can balance in this time of transition, the better the foundation for the new age. We may not know when karma is due, but God knows, and so does our Higher Self. And the law is unerring, unfailing and always just.

If we are spiritually wise, we will seek to sow good karma. We have many opportunities each day to serve life and uphold our responsibilities, doing all we can to help others and share our gifts. Our family, our community, our work and our profession are important means of doing this.

At the same time, we seek to balance returning negative karma. The universe often brings right to our doorstep those we have known in previous lives and whom we can now serve in balancing a karmic debt. It often begins right within our family.

God has given us free will in this universe and in our lives. We have a lot of latitude to do as we please. But free will operates within boundaries. Even in the physical plane, we are all subject to the laws of nature. If we made a free will choice to try and float through the air, we would soon experience the law of gravity. If we understand this law, we can avoid suffering because we won't step off high buildings.

In the same way, we all must live with the law of karma. If we understand it, we can avoid a lot of pain. We will understand that in the exercise of free will, we make choices that will determine what will come next in our life, whether blessing or bane, joy or sorrow—according to what we have sown. If you are an observer of life, you will readily see how this law is always acting.

In the New Testament we read, "God is not mocked. Whatsoever a man soweth that shall he also reap." This means that we can't ignore God's law of karma or think that it does not apply to us. Whatever we send out must eventually come due.

If at the conclusion of a lifetime we wind up with many karmic debts still to be paid, God, in his mercy, gives us the chance to return and make things right. Re-embodiment is a great opportunity. It also is a merciful solution when compared with the idea that it's either heaven or hell at the end of one life. Realistically, most of us are probably ready for neither. Instead, we have the chance to come back again to finish our mission here on earth. And this is what we would most want to do.

Jesus had that great desire. He said, "I must work the works of him that sent me," and "The Father worketh hitherto and I work." We have also come to do the work of our Father and have a great desire to fulfill our own divine plan. Many people today have an inner sense of karma. Beyond karma is dharma—the fiery destiny of the soul, the desire to fulfill our reason for being.

Every soul who is prepared for rebirth is charged with that sense of completing unfinished business. We want to give the world something of ourselves. It might be a creative gift or a gift of love, sweetness and kindness. It might be a small act of charity or a monumental achievement. The gift each of us will lay upon the altar will vary according to our divine plan.

A Glimpse into the
Spiritual Life of the Unborn

We find confirmation of some of these spiritual truths in the fascinating work of Dr. Helen Wambach, a clinical psychologist and regression therapy expert who pioneered past-life and pre-natal research. Her studies give a glimpse into the spiritual life of the unborn child and the continuity of the soul. She once said of her work: "Ninety percent of the people who come to me definitely flash on images from a past life."

In one study, she asked 750 people under hypnosis questions about their life before birth. She analyzed their answers in her book *Life before Life*.[1] Although hypnosis can be dangerous under certain circumstances and is not recommended for those on a spiritual path,[2] Dr. Wambach's findings are worthy of study. They reveal the soul's sense of the timetable of its mission.

Many of her subjects knew they were born in the twentieth century for a specific reason, and the majority of these said they chose this time period "because of its great potential for spiritual growth."

Thirty percent of Dr. Wambach's subjects knew they had to live during this time in order to be with certain people. Some stated that their purpose in this lifetime "was to be with one or several other people they had known in past lives in order to work out their relationships." Others said they had come to fulfill a certain mission.

Dr. Wambach observed that "the largest group of the sample said that the purpose of this lifetime was to grow spiritually and to teach others." One of her subjects said,

"Before my birth there was a conference, and I had a feeling of deep love from one of my advisers. He talked of my yearning to reach my life plan. When you asked about purpose, all I felt was a strong feeling of a plan." Her subjects agreed that "others helped them in the process of choosing another lifetime." Of those who reported having counselors before birth, fifty-nine percent mentioned more than one counselor.

We all have spiritual counselors in heaven who groom us for our soul's encounter with the challenge of our karma in our next life— they are known as Lords of Karma or the Karmic Board of Spiritual Overseers.

Between embodiments and while in the womb, the soul is busy preparing for life's challenges. The soul is tutored by spiritual beings on what is called the etheric plane, an aspect of the heaven world. It is as real and concrete as the physical plane but is experienced through the senses of the soul in a dimension and consciousness beyond physical awareness. Those who have been through a near-death experience report that the etheric plane does indeed feel more "real" than the real world.

The etheric plane is a vast and complex world. There we find ascended masters, angels and great beings of light. When souls of light are without a physical body between embodiments, they often reside in this dimension of being. Here they are schooled in etheric retreats and universities of the spirit by angels and masters.

While your physical body is in the sleep state, you also have the opportunity to travel in your finer bodies to the etheric plane to receive lessons from your elder brothers and sisters, the ascended masters. You may not consciously remember these experiences, but they are very real. Some people have glimpses of their experiences at inner levels through their soul memory or their dreams. Sometimes the door to realms of light, our real and eternal home, opens just a crack, and we can peep through.

Before coming into embodiment, each soul passes before the Lords of Karma to receive the assignments for that life. We may have many promises to keep and assignments to fulfill. They are specific to each soul. Some assignments are karma carried over from previous lives. Some are new assignments and new opportunities. There are weeds to pull and flowers to plant in our "garden" here on earth.

The Sensitivity of the
Child in the Womb

*D*r. Wambach's study also reveals the heightened sensitivity of the child in the womb. She reported that 86 percent of her subjects said "they became aware of the feelings, emotions and even thoughts of their mother before they were born." They were also aware of their mother's interactions with their father. They could sense their mother's many different emotions—from fear and anger to peace and well-being. If the mother became angry or upset, this would also burden the child. From these first-hand accounts, there is no doubt that the child in the womb knows his mother, hears her words and can become comforted or frightened by what is heard and sensed.

One woman relates a tragic example. One day during her pregnancy, she had become very angry with her husband. She flew into an intense and prolonged rage. The next day she had a miscarriage, and she knew, deep within her soul, that she had caused the miscarriage by her rage. Sadly, either the child had elected not to be born through them, or the energy was so intense that it actually killed the fetus.

This story illustrates the need to be careful about one's emotions while carrying a child. Just as with a newborn, the child in the womb is sensitive to her parents and their emotions.

Of course, not all miscarriages are due to the inharmonious emotions of the parents. A miscarriage may take place when all is not well with the embryo or when the soul considers that the body being prepared is not suitable. A miscarriage may also occur because of the mother's negligence in the care of her body or her diet or through participation in activities that might harm the developing child.

Often, however, a miscarriage is God's merciful solution to a situation in which the physical vessel would not have been adequate and viable for the incoming soul to complete her mission. If we do our best to nurture life and a miscarriage takes place, then it is in the hands of God. We commend the soul unto God and hope that we can bear another child at another time, if it is his will.

Adoption—Is It by Chance?

One interesting finding of Dr. Wambach's research concerns adoption. Some of her subjects said they knew before they were born that they were going to be adopted. She says, "Some of them knew before they were born of the relationship they would have with their adoptive parents and felt that they would not be able to come to them as their own genetic child but chose the method of adoption as a way to reach their parents."

She concluded that "chance and accident apparently played no part in adoption." This confirms what many spiritual teachers have said—there are no accidents for the birth parents, for the adoptive parents or for the child. It could be that a woman may only need to give birth to a child to balance her karma with that lifestream. She may then be able to offer the child to other parents, who were intended from the beginning to be the ones who would care for and love the child as their own.

Truly, the pregnancy would not have occurred if God had not ordained the conception of the child. Not one birth has ever taken place in this world that was not sanctioned by Almighty God and the Holy Spirit. For where there is conception, there is the divine hand and the divine will.

These concepts are life changing if shared with parents who feel unready or are unwilling to raise a child and may be thinking of abortion. We can love and care for the prospective mother, especially if she is unwed. We can teach her to love her baby in the womb and encourage her to carry her child to term. If she hears the story of the life of the

il in the womb, she might choose to give the
ld for adoption if she has to, knowing that
: child can be in its right place and pursue
divine plan. In this way, parents make good
rma by bringing that child into the world
her than negative karma in aborting it.

There is no such thing as an unwanted
ld. *God* loves every child.

God loved you in the beginning, has loved
u through the burdens of life, and will love
u all the way to your return home to his
art. And, although parents may not want
ir children here on earth, there need not be
wanted children, for there are so many par-
:s who desire to receive them.

In heaven there are no unwanted children.
nen earth rejects them, the angels receive
m back into their home of love and light. 🕊

The Role of the Parents in the Timetable of the Soul

*B*efore conception, the parents of ev
child—whether or not they are aware
it in their outer consciousness—have agr
on the inner to receive that soul. Or, if t
have not agreed, they have been given
understanding that receiving this being is r
essary to balancing a certain karma.

Sometimes parents do not want to face
responsibility (just as there are some who
not want to pay their debts). Often, thi
because their parents, teachers, pastors, mi
ters and rabbis have not known of the cy
of life and karma and could not teach w
they did not know. They have not taught th

at if they do not fulfill their calling to bear
e, they will, in a sense, be aborting their own
e plan and its cycles.

So, in resisting the assignment to receive a
ild and by not taking the opportunity to bal-
ce the karma with that child, parents may
ace themselves in an even more difficult cir-
mstance. Sometime, somewhere, they may
t have to bear that child. And not having
lanced this karma, they may find that the
cles of their own life are thrown off-track,
d they cannot proceed with their own divine
an. Their own spiritual progress can become
nited or even stop. In denying life, their own
e plan may be denied. And it may be very
fficult to come to the place once again where
e same two individuals will be together and
at same soul will be available and blessed by
od to take embodiment. The ties of karma
e often binding until they are dissolved, and
metimes karmic ties may require a couple to
ncarnate again in order to give birth to the

child who was denied opportunity.

This is why it is wise to respect the opportunity God gives us to bear children. We can rejoice in the opportunity of giving life to those from whom sometime, somewhere we may have taken life. This is a great joy and one of the purposes of marriage—the bringing forth of children who can carry on in their mission, even as through them we are allowed to fulfill our mission.

Our first children are often those to whom we owe a debt of karma. Later, parents who have already had children and balanced the karma they needed to in this way may be given the opportunity to bring forth other children with whom they have no negative karma. These may be highly gifted children who may make a great contribution to society as they bring their past attainment with them. 🕊

Abortion from a Spiritual Perspective

When a father and a mother abort their child, they are aborting a living potential that is in that child from the moment of conception. The child in the womb—and the soul who is already a part of that body—has consciousness, has awareness of its mother and father, and looks forward to being born and fulfilling its mission in life. This is the most profound reason why abortion is against the law of God and always has been.

When we understand the continuity of the soul, we realize that the "child-man" in the womb is a mature soul having complete thoughts and deep feelings. Only the body undeveloped. The baby's body, the greatest miracle of God's gift of love to man and woman, is a new house that the soul will enter and integrate with during the period from conception to birth. The soul, attached to this fragile form, pleads for entrance to life at the portals of birth, yet she is defenseless and at the mercy of her parents and society.

No matter what the argument, from a spiritual perspective, a new life has begun at the moment of conception. At that point, the Spirit begins to weave itself as part of the fabric of the developing body in the womb—a unique soul, a unique DNA, a unique potential.

God doesn't simply stuff a soul into a body like you stuff a pillow into a pillowcase. The integration of the soul with the developing body is a complex process.

This process, in fact, continues after birth. As the child grows in grace and waxes strong in the spirit, as Jesus did, the Christ consciousness descends into that temple, incre-

ment by increment, year by year. Thus, there
a continuum, and the integration of the sou
with the body and the soul with the High
Self takes place from the moment of concep
tion, continuing throughout adulthood.

An unborn baby, as you can see, is not ju
a product of conception, another part of i
mother's body or a lump of tissue.

A baby is life—life aborning in the womb

Myths and Arguments
about Abortion

The concepts of karma and reincarnation give a new understanding of life and the nique destiny of each child in the womb. Iowever, an incomplete understanding of arma and reincarnation has been used by ome to justify abortion. Here are some of hese erroneous concepts:

Myth:
The soul can always come back in another body.

Orthodox Hindus, Buddhists and Sikhs elieve in rebirth. They also believe that abor- on is taking life. Every sect of Hinduism holds at the soul enters the fetus at the moment of

conception. Today, however, many adherents o
these faiths believe abortion is permissibl
because they think it will not deprive a soul o
her one and only chance at life. They surmis
that the soul can always come back in anothe
body.   In an extension of this argument, som
contend that a woman's freedom of choic
should take precedence over the baby's righ
to life because the baby will always hav
another chance.

The idea that a soul has complete freedoı
to choose her experiences ignores the law o
karma. We certainly do have free will, and w
have been exercising it for many lifetimes. B
our past choices we have created the karm
circumstances that require our return in a sp
cific body, at a specific time and at a specif
place through specific parents. We can't ju
choose to enter life whenever we feel like it o
wherever we want to or with whomever w
might choose as parents. We have cycles ı
fulfill, and there are important consequences

hese cycles are missed.

Furthermore, if souls could choose their bodies, wouldn't most people choose to be brilliant, beautiful and wealthy? And yet we know that everyone isn't brilliant, beautiful and wealthy.

Many Americans take this one step further. They do not believe the soul is in the body during gestation, and, therefore, they conclude that there is nothing wrong with abortion.

In fact, the soul *is* in the body during gestation, and, although it may come and go, it is intimately connected to the developing body.

Myth:
The fetus is energy, and energy cannot be killed.

Some argue that the fetus is energy and therefore cannot be killed. By that same argument, taking the life of an adult could also be condoned because "a person is energy" and energy cannot be killed."

We all know at a soul level that taking life

is wrong, and we would not want our own lif
opportunity to be denied. The Creator ha
locked the energy of the fetus into physica
form, and that form is more than mere energ
coalesced. It is a child-man made in the imag
and likeness of God.

Myth:
The soul chooses her experiences.
If a child is aborted, it must have been
the choice of the soul.

Some suggest that a soul may choose t
experience life in the womb for a few month
and then return to higher octaves after a
abortion. In some cases it may be the choice o
the soul, or even the dictate of karma, for
child to be in the womb only a short time.

However, there are ways for God or th
soul to bring this about, and this can be see
in some cases of miscarriage. When th
occurs, it is according to the timetables set b
God—not man. How can we judge whe
someone's time on earth should end?

The Preexistence of the Soul

*W*hen does the soul enter the bo
Most orthodox Christians believe t
a brand-new soul is created for every n
embryo.

We understand, however, that the s
does exist before conception. The soul i
continuum—it existed in the beginning w
God. As we are created, the soul comes fo
out of the great white-fire ovoid of light. *T*
soul then descends into material form to fu
its reason for being.

New souls are indeed created, and t
must often complete many life cycles
embodiment before they can return to t

int of origin. When the soul exercises right oices, there is an increase of light in the ra, and the soul gains in self-mastery in der to one day return home to the temples of ht.

The confirmation of the preexistence of the ul is even found in the Bible. When God oke to the prophet Jeremiah he said: "Before ormed thee in the belly I knew thee; and fore thou camest forth out of the womb I nctified thee, and I ordained thee a prophet to the nations." God had predestined the ul of Jeremiah, just as he has predestined ur soul to go forth to fulfill a mission of lendor, light, usefulness and creativity in this rth and throughout the spheres of the heav-s.

But just as the traditional Christian view is nting, so is that of some in the New Age ovement. The belief of modern reincarna-nists, that aborting the body is acceptable cause it's only a body, is a denial that the body is the temple of the living God. The apostle Paul said, "What? Know ye not that your body is the temple of the Holy Ghost which is in you, which ye have of God, and are not your own? For ye are bought with a price: therefore glorify God in your body, and in your spirit, which are God's. Ye are the temple of the living God; as God hath said, I will dwell in them, and walk in them; and I will their God, and they shall be my people."

Our bodies are the dwelling places of Holy Ghost, and even the opportunity have for life and soul evolution is ours because of the sacrifices of the saints and great beings of light who have gone before us. And, ultimately, it is the light of God that has created us and sustains us each day.

Therefore, our bodies are not our own. Even our souls are not our own. There is personal ownership of the body—only personal stewardship.

God has created us and ordained us

bring forth souls made in his image and like
ness. God has ordained us to be co-creator
with him, not above him.

Life in the womb is life at the moment o
conception.

Life must be protected.

Life has the right to come forth.

Paul explains that there is a responsibilit
that comes with the life we have received. Par
of that responsibility is to defend other part
of life.

We may think that we are free to choose no
to bring forth the soul that has been conceived
But the soul is already in the womb, attached t
that body from the moment of conception. An
the decision as to whether to bring forth tha
life, in fact, does not belong to us. 🕊

We Are Spiritual Beings
with a Physical Body

*E*ach one of us has a soul, and that soul has awareness. That awareness is called solar awareness or solar consciousness. Our soul is like the sun in the heavens—our spiritual awareness is spherical, not linear. It is a continuing awareness from the hour of our point of origin in our going out from God until our return. Our solar awareness is integral to every part of our body—our arms, our fingers, our eyes, our nose, our every organ and even our finer bodies.

We are not just our physical bodies. We are magnificent spiritual beings who happen to have a physical body. We also have other vehicles for our soul's expression. We think and feel and have emotions. In fact, we are spiritual beings with four bodies in the planes of matter, including the physical body. We have a memory body, a mental body and a desire body as well as the physical body. We can suffer not only the anguish of physical pain but also the agony of emotional pain. Our physical organs can actually become ill because of the pain of the soul.

More happens during gestation than just the soul meshing with the physical body. From the moment of conception, the child's soul is an active participant in forming the body she is to inhabit to fulfill her mission in life.

Throughout the entire nine months of gestation, the soul may go back and forth from her body in the womb to higher planes of existence in the heaven-world. Each time the soul enters her body, she anchors more of her soul substance in that body. As gestation progresses, the spirit, or the essence, of the soul

life. We all have to deal with these desires
sort them out, choosing which ones we
retain and which ones we will let go.

Which desires shall we fulfill in this
time? This we learn with the help and g
ance of teachers, parents and our commur
with our own inner God. Many times our
memory of the training we received before
embodiment helps us to focus and channel
energy and efforts according to the divine
for our life.

In order to function in the earthly re
we all have to explore and consider what
we want to accomplish in life. What are
unfulfilled goals?

For instance, if in previous incarnat
our lifestream was suddenly, perhaps vio
ly, cut off or came to an end in the flus
youth or the prime of life, all that we
wanted to do with our life came to an en
well. We may desire to come back and pic
the pieces right where we left off. We

e a great desire to be reunited with former
ed ones as soon as possible and to fulfill the
n that we began in that former life. We feel
urgency of needing to have a physical body
order to do the things that we came on
th to do.

During one lifetime, just a slice of the
lity of our being will become prominent.
eality, our life is infinite, and it cannot all
expressed in one incarnation, and certainly
in this earthly realm. For this finite time-
-space world, this finite body, cannot con-
the totality of our being.

For example, part of a soul's divine plan
be to uplift the world through music. The
may have had several embodiments in
ch music came to the fore and brings with
when she is born the ability to compose.
he child grows, we marvel at how easily he
he learns music and just "knows" how to
an instrument. In fact, the child is effort-
y tapping into the attainment of past lives.

In a future embodiment, music may placed on the "back burner" if the s assignment is to work on bringing forth o aspects of being. Perhaps excelling in ma matics or architecture will help the child le different soul lessons. Or the soul may intended to bring forth members of a fa and help those souls develop certain s These are not unlikely scenarios.

The soul knows there are specific ass ments that must be fulfilled so she can l the lessons of love and complete the u ished business of life. Parents can provide opportunity for the soul to learn what needs and to prepare for her mission.

At levels of pre-conception, while pre ing to take embodiment, the soul is instru in these and other concepts in schools of l retreats of the ascended masters in the et octaves. She is tutored for her mission prepared to win a victory, perhaps not jus the upcoming life but for all her lives on e

ich would free her from the rounds of rein-
nation to ascend back into the arms of her
her-Mother God.

Many of us are here today because we
e unfinished business. We have many
gs we want to do. One of the most impor-
concepts to grasp about the soul in the
nb is the tremendous opportunity it pre-
s for the fulfillment of a destiny ordained
God.

The unborn child is developing and contin-
to develop after birth. In the womb, the
, the spirit, the mind and the desire body are
grating with the new physical body, the new
d and the new opportunity that this life
gs. And life goals begin to clarify and take
e as the focus sharpens on what will be. 🕊

The Seed of Immortality
within and the Need to Sacrifice

It has been argued that the fetus is n
human being, only a *potential* hu
being—hence, abortion is permissible. Bu
we ever say that someone should be subje
elimination because he has not realized hi
human or divine potential? Which of u
yet realized all that we are intended to b

Each of us has the unlimited possibil
realize the seed of God, the seed of Life

Yes, we have had the seed of our in
tality even prior to conception. We
always had that seed, for immortality i
goal and the reason God sent us into inc
tion. We don't say to one another, "Well,

THE SEED OF IMMORTALITY WITHIN

you, or you, or you because you're not a
d yet; you're just a potential God."

At what stage of physical/spiritual evolu-
1 do we draw the line?

Consider even the physical consequences
eliminating a single human being: We
uld be eliminating a link in the genetic
in, and this chain could ultimately bring
:h a Beethoven, a Shakespeare, a
:helangelo, an Einstein, an Abraham
:oln, a Jesus Christ, a Buddha or any of the
showers and geniuses who have enabled
ianity to leap forward scientifically, cultur-
and spiritually.

The common man is also a carrier of the
:s of genius that may one day appear in the
n of evolution. We all have a divine spark
n us by our God, and we are sons and
;hters of God.

)ur civilization currently does not consid-
aat life necessitates sacrifice, but, from a
tual perspective, it does. The bearing of

children is a sacrifice as well as a surren
unto God and unto our divine calling.

Many couples feel called to give birth
children and have a great desire to do so. T
have a great love for their children and l
forward to bringing them into the wo
Being parents is one of the most impor
callings in the world.

We may also have the divine calling
dharma³) and the karma to bring forth
because we have afflicted life in the past.
bring forth children because it is our resp
bility and because, by having children,
learn to love and to care for life.

Sadly, many women who abort childr
their teenage years and in their twenties
that they are not able to have children lat
life even though they may then greatly d
to be a mother to a child. They are often
rowful and burdened because they feel lif
passed them by. They feel they have misse
essential element of their divine plan, and

can be true.

Instead of having opted for abortion, they could have borne the child and given it for adoption or else cared for it. No matter which option they chose, through personal sacrifice they could have balanced and fulfilled the karma of giving life to that child. ✒

The Awareness and
the Pain of the Soul

*A*bortion affects the unborn child in many ways. Whether a child in the womb feels pain as it is being aborted is hotly debated. Let us consider this as well as the deeper question of whether the soul experiences pain.

The soul that occupies first the embryo, then the fetus, then the full-term baby in the womb has awareness—the soul or "solar" awareness that we spoke of previously. The soul also has sensitivity through the spiritual senses.

There are five spiritual senses that correspond to our five physical senses. They are what give some people a heightened psychic-

or soul-sensitivity. Everyone has them, but not everyone develops them. When they do, it is said they are psychic or intuitive or have a "sixth sense."

These senses give you a direct soul-knowledge of events and circumstances, even a precognition of what is to come. But they do not function entirely independent of the five senses, the brain, the physical heart or the central nervous system because we are an integrated personality in God before, during and after the nine months that we occupy our mother's womb.

The question, then, of when an unborn child feels pain cannot be answered without the understanding that the soul and spirit—with memory, mind and desires fully engaged—are experiencing life in all its multifaceted dimensions in and through the physical body—as well as independently of it.

Sensory perception and extrasensory perception go hand in hand. The fetus (and the soul through and in the fetus), made in the image and likeness of God, experiences life as a complex whole.

Whether or not sensory nerves are fully developed and functioning in the fetus is not the determining factor. That determining factor is to be discovered in the *sum* of the parts.

It is like trying to examine a rose to see how it's put together and where the beautiful perfume comes from. When you take it apart, petal by petal, you have destroyed the very thing that you desired to understand—the beauty of the rose.

An unborn child experiences life in all its richness—as we do. Would it not, then, experience pain as we do?

How do we feel pain?

Just as we feel pleasure with all of our being, so we feel pain. If you have ever suffered intense pain in any part of the body, you know that it affects your entire body. Pain is an all-pervasive, all-consuming experience.

It is the person—the soul, the mind, the being and, yes, the body—as one individual whole who is fully aware of pain and pleasure. This is true even in the womb!

You sucked your thumb in your mother's womb as early as nine weeks. (An ultrasound can show a baby sucking its thumb.) Why would you have sucked your thumb if you had not derived gratification from it, if you had not wanted to satisfy physical and emotional urges and needs? And in what dimensions of being do pain and pleasure begin and end?

Just as the soul of the child in the womb comes and goes during gestation, so your soul journeys to higher octaves in the heaven-world while you sleep. But during your soul travel, a portion of your soul substance remains with the body, for it is meshed with the mind, the cells and the organs. This explains why, when you are abruptly awakened in the middle of the night, you're a bit groggy at first and then become more and more focused as your soul fully re-enters the body.

If you were to be violently murdered during sleep and your soul was suddenly in another plane, you would still experience intense physical and emotional trauma through all your physical and spiritual faculties. Is it any different for a child aborted in the womb? No!

An unborn child is, from the moment of its conception, a complete, multifaceted human being and a son or daughter of God. What may be lacking in fetal development is not lacking in the awareness of the soul, who abides for a time in the womb, preparing to take up her God-ordained destiny in the world of form.

If we can't even answer these kinds of questions, we would be wise to leave to the Almighty to work the miracle of life within the womb of creation. 🕊

The Pain of Abortion

*U*ntil recently, it was thought that the fetus and the newborn were not capable of feeling pain. Medical evidence, however, now tells us that the unborn child may feel pain as early as seven weeks and definitely feels pain at five to six months.

Each year in America 30 percent of all women who become pregnant abort their children. By the eighth week the baby has tiny hands with five fingers, a permanent palm and his or her own unique fingerprints. And what is most important, he or she can feel pain.

By the end of the twelfth week, the baby has muscles and nerves, and virtually every part of his body responds to touch. He can squint and frown, kick and cry (although he makes no sound), swallow and digest amniotic fluid (the fluid which surrounds the baby in the womb). Although it is not conclusive evidence, we have only to look at an ultrasound showing how a twelve-week-old fetus struggles to avoid the surgical instruments during a suction abortion—which will literally tear it to pieces—to conclude that the first-trimester fetus both feels and fears pain.

It may be hard to hear these words, but they need to be said. Souls who are trying to embody on earth today enter their mother's womb courageously facing the reality that they could be torn from it. We need to face this same reality.

In most cases, those who abort their children do not know that the unborn child experiences physical pain during the procedure. The masters teach that the child in the womb who is aborted does indeed go through the pain of abortion. This knowledge alone could have a tremendous impact on people who are deciding whether to abort their child. Most people are just not given these facts when the life of their child is at stake and destinies hang in the balance.

It is sad beyond belief to realize that the child does suffer a horrible death. And the death is suffered in silence.

The abortion of body, spirit and soul in the womb is violence unutterable and unimaginable—a crucifixion of our children.

After an abortion, the angels come to comfort the child, who is in shock and pain. Healing angels bear the soul, bruised and beaten, to temples of light where she is consoled, cared for, healed and prepared for the next level of spiritual evolution.

The child who is aborted is deeply scarred. Somewhere, sometime, those scars must be healed in successive embodiments. 🕊

The Pain of Not Being in Embodiment

At inner levels, souls who have been denied life feel a tremendous anguish and frustration that they are not in embodiment. And this suffering may be an even greater agony than the pain of the abortion itself. They long to be cradled by mothers and fathers, and they mourn the lost opportunity to be with their families.

These souls want to take their place in the great cosmic scheme of life. They want to fulfill their mission, offer their gifts to the world, help us meet the crises in the cities and nations—yet they are not in embodiment to serve humanity.

In many cases, the desire of souls to be a part of the divine plan of earth is so great that they volunteer to re-embody again and again knowing that they face the risk of repeated abortion.

When these valiant souls make it into embodiment again, they may carry the burden of coping with the emotional and psychological scars of having been aborted. This can manifest in childhood or later life as an unexplained depression or an emotional or physical illness. They may resent their parents or others who have aborted them. These wounded souls are in need of love and healing. 🕊

The Abortion of a Divine Plan
from the Child's Perspective

*F*rom the soul's point of view, the most
painful and tragic consequence of abortion is that it aborts the divine plan—the special mission in life they have been waiting to
fulfill, sometimes for thousands of years.

All of us have dates to keep, dates with our
destiny and with our karma. If we miss the
dates to pay off old debts, if we don't catch the
cycles to fulfill our mission, these windows of
opportunity may not open again for a long,
long time—perhaps for a span of time that
seems unimaginable.

Abortion can also jeopardize or derail the
missions of mandalas of souls—groups of souls

who are tied together by their karma and cannot complete their mission because part of their "team" did not make it into embodiment.

Since the 1973 Supreme Court decision of Roe v. Wade, more than 40 million abortions have been performed in the United States alone—an equivalent of 14 percent of the current U.S. population—and between 1 billion and 1.5 billion children have been aborted worldwide.

One seventh of the people who are meant to be in the world are missing, and souls who need to reincarnate to balance karma are finding it increasingly difficult to do so. 🕊

The Emotional, Physical and Spiritual Effects of Abortion on the Parents

*A*bortion does not just affect the child. It can also have lasting impacts on the parents. One obvious effect is on the physical health of the mother.

Testimony before the United States Congress in 1983 included a report that twenty to thirty percent of all abortions performed in hospitals cause long-lasting negative effects, primarily involving reproduction and fertility. A 1986 study of the effect of abortion on subsequent pregnancies showed that "forceful dilatation of the cervix by any procedure, whether in a first or second trimester abortion, predisposes a subsequent pregnancy to increased risk."

Other studies indicate that the abortion of a first pregnancy causes complications with future pregnancies, increases the chances of miscarriage in the first and second trimester and increases the chances of premature births and deaths among newborns. When the cervix, uterine wall, or delicate fallopian tubes are harmed, the risks increase for ectopic pregnancies,[4] infertility and other problems in labor, delivery and carrying a pregnancy to term.

There is a definite link between abortion and infertility. An increasing number of women are dealing with infertility after abortions early in life. This has many implications.

For example, often a child who has been aborted may want to re-embody in that same family at a later time, when the parents are ready to accept a baby. But, sadly, a mother who has aborted a child may find that, due to infertility, she is unable to have the child she now desires. Although the parents and the child all now desire to fulfill their mission, the soul still finds the way barred.

The complications of abortion for a woman are not limited to physical effects. In the aftermath of an abortion, many women must deal with the emotional consequences of knowing that they have taken a life. The after-effects of abortion are called Post Abortion Syndrome.

A woman may suppress her responses to the abortion for years. One counselor who treats women with Post Abortion Syndrome says, "The crisis point occurs most often between two and five years after the abortion. For some women, the crisis may come within months of the abortion. For others, repression may last twenty to thirty years or more."

The most common symptoms can include guilt, anxiety, depression, intense grief, anger, suicidal urges, drug and/or alcohol abuse, sexual problems, nightmares, lowered self-esteem and development of eating disorders.

Although no one knows for certain how

prevalent psychological problems are among women who have had abortions, for some, the effects have been devastating. One doctor and psychiatrist who performed thousands of abortions says: "There is no question about the emotional grief and mourning following an abortion. It shows up in various forms. I've had patients who had abortions a year or two before—women who did the best thing at the time for themselves—but it still bothers them. Many burst out crying. A psychological price is paid."

And so we find that women are not liberated through abortion, nor do they gain the freedom they longed for. They often suffer greatly and can become enslaved to a pain that is not physical.

In addition to the emotional pain, there is an even deeper spiritual pain that, in many cases, gnaws at a woman for the rest of her life—even in future incarnations—until it is resolved. Many who had an abortion can witness to this profound spiritual pain.

One doctor testifies, "I saw many women who had not only physical problems after abortions but also psychological and emotional problems, many of which were fairly deep-seated. I've had patients who had abortions even twenty, thirty years ago. When they came in for a regular pap smear, they would tell me that they had had an abortion twenty-five years ago and they still regret it to this day. And they would tell me about the gnawing pain."

One midwife says that when she is taking her patient's history of past surgeries, "Every woman who has had an abortion cries as she tells of the experience, even if it is ten years or more afterwards. They all vividly remember the experience and still live with the guilt, no matter who tells them to let go of the guilt. They have long-lasting regrets."

Just as the unborn child has a soul and soul awareness that are scarred during an abortion, so the mother has a soul and soul awareness. At a soul level she knows the reality of the situation and what it will mean for her. She knows what has happened to the child, and it deeply disturbs her, even if she is not aware of this in her outer mind.

Part of the anguish is also because every mother who chooses abortion is actually destroying a part of herself. Every father who chooses abortion is also destroying a part of himself. The part of them that is destroyed is a part of the self that will not be realized or fulfilled except through the fruition of those genes that exist in man and woman as human and as God-potential.

And there is yet another karmic consequence. According to karmic law, those associated with abortion—through having had an abortion or having performed them or having encouraged another to have an abortion—may in a future incarnation be denied entrance to the physical octave through the portals of birth.

Our hearts go out to those women who are suffering in the aftermath of an abortion. We can see how the woman who carries her baby to term and gives it a chance for life, regardless of whether she keeps the child or offers it for adoption, is better able to make her peace with life and with her baby.

Birth Control Begins
before Conception

*F*rom a spiritual perspective, birth control should begin before conception. Abortion should never be considered a form of birth control.

We agree that we ought not bring forth more children than we are able to care for and for whom we can adequately express our love. Yet, if we take a strictly economic view, Jesus Christ and Abraham Lincoln should never have been born, since both were born into poverty. But even from an economic point of view, we have the spiritual understanding that if God gives us children, he will usually give us the means to provide for them.

Bringing forth a child is a sacred responsibility, and birth control is a private matter. Family planning and the use of contraceptives are necessary and important, and better and better methods of birth control are available. Choose those that do not harm the mother. But, to repeat, from a spiritual perspective, abortion is not an acceptable form of birth control.

Adoption as an Alternative

*D*r. Helen Wambach's work gives a fascinating insight into the issue of adoption. Some of her subjects who were adopted children said that they knew *before* they were born that they would be adopted. It was part of their life plan.

Adoption is a spiritual solution to a spiritual dilemma. Although more complicated on the outer, adoption can bring to parents the same soul they would have received through the birth process.

There are adoption angels who work specifically on connecting prospective parents with the souls to whom they are meant to minister through parenthood. Their work is not simple, as free will can step in at any moment and reverse a situation that was meant to occur.

Some people worry about adopting the right soul. You will not get a soul that is not intended for you if you pray about all aspects of the adoption—starting before you begin the process and continuing until the child is in your arms. If something doesn't work out, even at the last moment, you must be at peace if you have done the necessary spiritual work.

Adoption is also one means of balancing the karma of abortion, although it may not be feasible or practical for everyone who wishes to adopt a child to do so. But rendering some type of service or support to a child, whether through financial donations or some other action, is a door open to most people. The avenue of prayer is, of course, available to all. Pray for clear direction for your families, and let your decisions be guided by the hand of God that never fails.

Mothers and fathers, if you do not want your children, please love them to term, and let them be born. Offer them for adoption to those who will love them and provide them with the opportunity once more to live and laugh and play and sing and work together with their friends on earth to fulfill their reason for being.

There are beautiful souls of light waiting to be adopted. There are also souls with challenging karma and momentums. The karma of the prospective parents will always be a part of the equation. Prospective parents would do well to pray always and use spiritual techniques to help transmute as much karma as possible before they adopt. 🕊

There Is Forgiveness after Abortion

Many people deeply regret their choices
regarding abortion. God in his infinite
mercy forgives and in his justice provides ways
to atone. God does not condemn us for our
ignorance or our lack of understanding, for,
truly, if we knew better, we would do better.

There is mercy and forgiveness and healing
after abortion. If you have aborted a child, do
not condemn yourself or abide in a sense of
unworthiness. This will do nothing for the
child, for you or for God. Instead, look for
ways to serve and honor life.

Involvement in abortion—whether you
had one, encouraged one, or performed them,

and whether or not you knew it was a sin at the time—will not prevent your returning to the heart of God in the ritual of the ascension in this lifetime if you give yourself to God in a service that can balance that karma.

Depending on your circumstances, you may have the opportunity to give birth to that soul (or to another soul if this option is not available). Adoption of a child may also be an alternative for you.

You may also be able to balance the karma through service to life, through sponsoring children, working with children, praying for the youth and through educating others about the spiritual issues of abortion.

The sin of abortion can be forgiven and it can be atoned for. *Atonement* means to balance the karma for a sin by your soul's at-one-ment with God.

There are prayers and other spiritual techniques that can greatly assist us in the balancing of karma and the healing of the emotional and spiritual traumas resulting from abortion. Many have found the violet flame to be an invaluable tool in overcoming these problems.

The Violet Flame
Smooths Relationships and
Transmutes Karma

The violet flame is a high-frequency spiritual energy that can be used to transmute, or change, negative karma into positive karma. In previous centuries, knowledge of the violet flame was given to only a few who had proven themselves worthy. These saints and adepts of East and West have long used the violet flame to accelerate their spiritual development, but this once-secret knowledge was not revealed to all of humanity until the twentieth century.

The violet flame revitalizes and invigorates us. It can heal emotional and even physical problems, improve relationships and make life easier. It works on the four lower bodies. By transforming negative thoughts and feelings, the violet flame provides a platform for healing. It can also be used to smooth the rough spots in relationships between mothers, fathers and their children. It is like oil in the gears that eases the way.

This transforming spiritual energy is called forth by the science of the spoken Word using mantras or worded formulas, called decrees, to anchor the violet flame into the physical plane. Like a cosmic eraser, it clears the cause and effect of negative karma, giving a new freedom and new opportunity to the soul.

The violet flame has been called the highest gift of God to the universe. Try it for yourself and for those you love. You may be very pleasantly surprised at the results.

Here is a simple affirmation that you can use each day to bring the transforming power of the violet flame into your life:

I AM a being of violet fire,
I AM the purity God desires.

The Vulnerability of the Nations

*B*eyond the effects on the individual, there are even wider ramifications of the practice of abortion. Each of us in our daily lives is affected, even those who have never had an abortion or been associated personally with abortion. In fact, the taking of life through abortion has resulted in a tremendous weight upon all of us.

What is perhaps most crucial is that the souls who have been aborted are not with us. These "missing persons" will not take their place as adults on the world scene in this century, nor will those who might have been their offspring. The absence of these souls in embodiment in this hour has compromised the divine plan for earth, and the karma that has been created by it is incalculable.

We are the losers, and this karma affects us all. It is a karma that weighs upon our entire civilization. If the sheer weight of this burden were lifted, we would all feel very different. Such an upset of the spiritual-cosmic ecosystem has not been seen upon earth since the last days of Atlantis. It has actually altered the course of civilization.

The millions of abortions that have been performed worldwide make America and the nations vulnerable to the return of negative karma.

One of the ways a civilization is judged is how it has cared for its young. We are responsible for our immediate families, but we are also a part of the family of God. From the perspective of heaven, abortion is the most pressing problem of our time because it is the greatest single transgression that causes the greatest karma for individuals and nations.

A key to turning back prophecy and staying all predictions concerning nuclear war and earth changes is, quite simply, the stopping of the practice of abortion. The heaven-world cannot adequately convey what a burden would be lifted from the planet if this practice would stop. Ending abortion is the key to our reprieve and the key to mercy flowing from the heart of Mother Mary, as she does intercede for the nations before the throne of grace.

The Laws of Universal Life

*T*hey say ignorance is bliss, but in the spiritual realm it doesn't work quite that way. The laws of the universe operate whether we are aware of them or not. And, unfortunately, many dear and lovely souls have been deceived into believing that abortion is a "right" or a lawful choice.

Free will is the gift of God to his sons and daughters. We are accountable for our decisions. If we decide to be sexually active, pregnancy is a possible consequence. Life is to be revered at all levels. The irony is that some people who honor the environment and are horrified by the destruction of planet Earth and fight for many species that are in jeopardy of extinction do not see that abortion is also the destruction of life, which is holy and meant to be protected.

Perhaps the most compelling understanding comes from the heaven-world itself. If you were to journey there, you would meet souls who have been denied embodiment not once but several times due to abortion. You would learn about abortion firsthand as they would tell you that they need the opportunity to advance spiritually, which requires that they re-embody. The soul is prepared to handle the situation no matter how difficult, and yet, if the parent decides to abort, the soul loses its opportunity.

Yes, God has given us free will. But does it seem likely that it is the will of God for us to take life? Yes, the rights of each individual are paramount. But individuality exists in consideration of the rights of others and the rights of the community. Individuality does not confer the right to take life.

And nature has always exacted a recompense for man's inhumanity to man. The truth is, a nation that has not defended life in the womb is vulnerable. And where the nation allows it and decrees it by law, so that nation becomes vulnerable.

Insensitivity to life in the womb breeds insensitivity to life everywhere. Spiritually speaking, it manifests in various ways. It can be the hardness or coldness of heart whereby one can ignore another's suffering. We can see it in the spiraling rates of crime and murder in cities around the world. It can result in unseasonable weather.

Who can say where it might manifest—in a spring blizzard or in the economy as an imbalance in supply or in households where brother is set against brother and there is division and hatred?

We can see it in the anger of nation rising up against nation. It is outpicturing in plague, pestilence or disease, in the increasing rates of cancer and AIDS upon the people of many nations.

At a soul level, we mourn for our brothers and sisters who are not with us—our soul mates and twin flames who are not at our side, those who were meant to be our partners in marriage or business or projects and enterprises for the betterment of mankind. We may succumb to these feelings or try to drown them out with lifestyles that are harmful to our bodies.

We all bear this heaviness in our bodies whether we know it or not. We feel it physically, emotionally, mentally and even spiritually. This heaviness manifests in subtle ways—in the rise in unexplained depressions, psychological problems, suicide, and alcohol and drug addictions that are increasing in the nations of the civilized world.

As a result of abortion, if we do not ascend back to God at the conclusion of our life, we may find it harder and harder to find parents through whom to re-embody on a safe and sane world.

Life must become sensitive to life. Human government since Noah has been founded to protect human life. The nation or the government that creates legislation allowing murder in the womb is doomed to go down unless it changes. It may go down by cataclysm. It may go down by economic collapse. But it *will* go down under the weight of its own karma, because the laws by which it has chosen to govern are not consistent with the laws of universal life.

And if individuals and nations must go through hardship to understand what they have been a part of, then the cosmic law does decree it. 🕊

Are There No Exceptions?
What about Rape and Incest?

Where there is a conception, there is the ordination of God for that life to come forth no matter what the circumstance. Abortion is only allowable spiritually when the life of the mother is in jeopardy.

Even if conception takes place by incest or rape, that conception is the will of God and must be hallowed—even though that life at its inception was not hallowed by the parents. It is God who sanctifies life, and even if the circumstances of conception were painful, that life can be sanctified and should not be denied.

This was brought home in a very poignant way in "Message from a Child of Rape: We

Don't Deserve to Die," an article by Michael Henderson in the *New York City Tribune* on October 4, 1990. It dealt with the painful subject of conception by rape.

Henderson tells the story of Julie Makimaa, a young, attractive and energetic Christian woman living in Michigan. Julie, an adopted child, desired to know the identity of her true parents. After four years of searching, she finally met her mother, Lee, who made the painful revelation that she had been conceived as the result of a rape at an office party. Lee had been an 18-year-old virgin at the time and was encouraged by friends to have the baby and place it with an adoption agency.

This message, rather than upsetting Julie, evoked a response of intense gratitude.

"I was very sorry that my mother had to go through that terrible experience," she said, "but I am so thankful that I am here. For me, I feel that it doesn't matter how I got here. What's important is what I do now."

Julie's husband told Lee: "I want to thank you for not aborting Julie. I don't know what my life would be like without her and my daughter."

Inspired by her mother's moral courage, Julie founded Fortress, an organization dedicated to defending women who become pregnant and children who were conceived through sexual assault.

There is an exception to the spiritual laws prohibiting abortion, and that is in the very specific instance in which the life of the mother is in danger. Thanks to modern medicine, these cases are very rare, but they do occur. In such a situation, abortion may be the decision that defends life most effectively—in this case, the life of the mother.

What About Those Who Are Born with Disabilities?

*E*very child that is conceived has a divine plan, a divine design. Some say that a child with a disability is "unwanted" or "handicapped," and, therefore, should not be born into this world. The renowned pediatric surgeon and former U.S. Surgeon General Dr. C. Everett Koop says, "It has been my constant experience that disability and unhappiness do not necessarily go together. Some of the most unhappy children whom I have known have all of their physical and mental faculties, and on the other hand, some of the happiest youngsters have borne burdens which I, myself, would find very difficult to bear."

We are all "handicapped" to some degree. We all have limitations and imperfections, and in old age these can become quite severe.

The point of life is not to be free of handicaps or free of burdens but to live the life that we have to the fullest, to be all we were meant to be, to accomplish the mission for which we took embodiment.

Who are we to say when a life is not worthwhile? Only God can make that decision.

Helen Keller proved that life is worth living and fighting for. How can we ever forget the remarkable determination and the daring of the deaf, dumb and blind girl who overcame the utter darkness of her childhood to become an exceptional author, educator and lecturer?

Public outrage over the death in 1982 of a baby boy with Down's syndrome illustrates this point. Infant Doe was born on Good Friday, April 9, 1982, with Down's syndrome—a genetic defect involving varying degrees of mental retardation and sometimes serious physical defects. It was the decision of his parents, upheld by the Indiana Supreme Court and their physician, to withhold food and medical treatment, allowing the child to die, because they believed their son would never be able to enjoy a "meaningful" life. To them, it was an act of love.

The baby boy died of starvation and dehydration on April 15, after an unsuccessful attempt by concerned citizens, working through the court system, to place him under the care of one of ten couples offering to adopt him.

On April 21, 1982, the *Los Angeles Times* published an editorial by George F. Will, "When Killing Becomes a Convenience," and a cartoon by Conrad, both commenting on Infant Doe.

Will wrote, "When a commentator has a direct personal interest in an issue, it behooves him to say so. Jonathan Will, 10, fourth-grader and Orioles fan (and the best Wiffle-ball hitter in southern Maryland), has Down's syndrome. He does not 'suffer from' (as newspapers are wont to say) Down's syndrome. He suffers from nothing, except anxiety about the Orioles' lousy start. He is doing nicely, thank you. But he is bound to have quite enough problems dealing with society—receiving the rights he is due, let alone empathy. He can do without people...asserting by their actions the principle that people like him are less than fully human."

The Conrad cartoon, entitled "They Shoot Horses Don't They?" depicts a skeleton-like baby lying in a hospital crib. A notation on the crib reads: "Rx for Down's Syndrome: Starvation." In a letter to the editor (*Los Angeles Times,* May 1), Donna Parun of San Pedro, California, wrote: "After cutting out the cartoon Conrad drew of the Down's syndrome baby starving to death in his crib, I left it on the kitchen table. My 10-year-old Down's syndrome son picked it up and looked at it. He likes to look at pictures. He said, 'Momma, a baby—me?' 'Yes,' I answered, 'he is like you, but I didn't let you starve to death.' He looked at me and said, 'Oh, why not?' He answers that to almost everything. I said, 'Because I love you, Matthew.' Smiling back, he said, 'I love you.' "

In response to public reaction over the tragic death of Infant Doe, President Ronald Reagan announced on April 30 that federal aid would be halted to any hospital or health care agency that withholds medical care from the handicapped.

People born into abject poverty and the worst of circumstances can rise to become great leaders who influence the destinies of nations. President Abraham Lincoln was born to uneducated parents and raised in a log cabin in the backwoods of Kentucky. The famous abolitionist leader Frederick Douglass was born and reared as a slave. American inventor and technological genius Thomas Edison attended school for only three months of his life because his schoolmaster thought he was retarded. Jesus Christ was born in a stable to parents who were, at least temporarily, homeless.

There is something higher than the body and the circumstances of birth. It is the drive of the soul and the spirit that gives character, direction and impetus to an individual.

Many people have serious karma. They may have committed appalling crimes in past lives such as murder and child abuse. Such individuals may be required by the law of their own karma to embody in circumstances that are not ideal. The purpose of karma is never to punish but to help us learn from our past mistakes, and sometimes the only way we can learn from past mistakes is to experience for ourselves what we have done to others.

The hard knocks of life are sometimes what our souls need to advance spiritually— not only through the expiation of karma but also through passing initiations and testings and making sacrifices.

The family and environment we are born into, the friends, the foes and the challenges we meet along life's way, are all a part of life's wondrous and intricate blueprint. This blueprint from the mind of God is given us so that we can overcome all things through Christ who strengthens us and, at the close of this incarnation, return home a graduate of earth's schoolroom.

Because modern religion in the West does not teach the principles of karma and reincarnation, people cannot have a true understanding of the many issues that our society faces. To eliminate pain and suffering at the price of the soul's evolution is not the wisdom of the laws of God. The soul must learn the lessons of karma. If she is denied these opportunities, she may be left without the necessary ingredients for her wholeness and return to God.

Even if it is foreknown that a child will be born with certain handicaps and difficulties, that child has a right to live to expiate its karma through being in that body.

Remember, too, that the situation may not be due to karma at all. Some highly advanced souls volunteer to take incarnation in a handicapped body as a sacrifice for others. If the fetus is aborted because it is not physically perfect, the lives this soul was meant to help must now do without her love and without her sacrifice on their behalf.

Indeed, the soul may even be a Christ or a lightbearer of Buddhic attainment who offered to enter the physically imperfect body to help the earth with the expiation of world karma.

When an abortion is recommended or sought because the fetus is "imperfect," how can anyone know whether this is a soul who is coming into embodiment to satisfy all remaining karma and then take her ascension? How can anyone know whether a Christ is coming into the world, only to be crucified in the womb?

If the child is given up for adoption, others will have the opportunity to care for it. In so doing, they may also nurture in their own hearts the mercy flame by ministering to a child who is not physically perfect.

It is best to let God determine what is to manifest and let parents truly enter the role of being parents. Certain conditions are genetic, and certain conditions are karmic. Yet some of these karmic conditions also may be alleviated by the mercy of the father and the mother who have gained wisdom and become wise in understanding what is the correct body chemistry and, therefore, the correct support for life in the womb.

The circumstances of life are for learning the lessons of life. God is teaching us in many ways, including experience and karma. We cannot just learn out of books. We are drawn from life, and to life we must go for some of our most essential lessons.

If We Knew Better, We Would Do Better

Many beautiful souls make the decision to abort their babies in total ignorance about what they are doing. If they had a correct understanding, they might make different choices.

A woman may decide to have an abortion for several reasons. She may feel that she is not ready for the responsibility of parenthood and that having a child would alter her life plans. She may be afraid for her reputation and the reaction of family and friends. If she already has children, she and her partner may feel that they cannot care for another child. Others may feel that the planet is overpopulated and do not wish to add to the numbers. Some are forced to have abortions by close family members or even political regimes.

Many, but not all, people make the decision to abort with a heavy heart and after much thought. But they still do so without an understanding of reincarnation and karma and with very little faith in God's abundance and the possibility that solutions can be found for everything when one asks fervently for divine intervention.

Truly, most of these decisions, if we really are honest, are based on some degree of selfishness and self-love. Hard as it is to face, they are ultimately decisions for human convenience and personal reputation.

If people knew the laws of karma and realized the importance of every soul who takes embodiment, they might rise above all other considerations and make very different choices.

Every soul needs a body in which to work out her karma. The soul selects the family that will best allow her to fulfill that karma. If parents decide to have an abortion, the soul they abort may have to wait a very long time for another opportunity with a different family—or may at a later date be born to the same person. But this time, the child may bring along an added layer of resentment or sense of conflict as a direct result of the abortion.

To have such an understanding is to come face-to-face with a cosmic truth that everyone needs to understand: No matter what the argument, life begins at conception, and, therefore, life in the womb should not be destroyed.

The Divine Solution

The solution to abortion *does not* lie in threatening or killing abortion providers or in making threats against abortion clinics. It *does not* lie in finger-pointing or in blaming anyone, ourselves included.

We will never find answers in hate, blame and violence.

Instead, we can find a higher way. The solution is compassionately providing a safe haven for the parents and their children.

We, individually and as communities, can support single mothers and mothers-to-be. We can also encourage mothers to carry their babies to term and, if they do not wish to raise them, to offer them for adoption. There are thousands and thousands of couples eagerly awaiting the opportunity to adopt a child.

We can also pray that souls who have been aborted and waiting to incarnate will find parents to sponsor them, give birth to them and love them. Those who are able to have children may provide a home for souls waiting to take their place on the stage of life. Many parents, especially those who understand the spiritual equation, can offer to give birth to not one but several children, so that they might bring in those who have been denied.

Those who have supported abortion or taken part in it and want to balance that karma should realize that God is merciful and has given us a way to become sponsors of life. We can rectify our karma not only through prayer work but also by giving birth to children or by adopting or sponsoring children financially. We can participate in community programs, become a mentor, or support organizations that care for underprivileged children or children and orphans in other nations, such as Tibet.

We are all part of the family of God upon earth, and we can pray for one another. We can pray for wisdom and understanding for all people so that they can understand why abortion is harmful to the child, to the parents and to us all. We can pray for healing for all souls who have been aborted. We can pray for the protection of life in the womb. We can pray for our leaders to make right choices even as we can pray for parents of children and those who are carrying new life in the womb to make right choices. We can pray that the unborn are able to be born and to take their rightful place on the stage of life.

On far-off worlds, the Buddhas of the light hear the cry of every little one. They know every cry, including the cry of pain from souls who have been aborted. The Buddhas go to each wounded baby, bow and enter the heart of the small one, saying, "Little child, you will not cry alone. We will be with you until all life does atone for this sin against thy soul, who is God."

Life, in all its complexity and wonder, is our greatest teacher, our greatest gift. If we support Life, revere Life, defend Life, we will all be blessed by Life in return.

Notes

Portions of the text on pages 75-77, 78, 84, 86-87 and 103-05 are excerpted and adapted from Patricia Kirmond, *Messages from Heaven,* (Corwin Springs, Mont.: Summit University Press, 1999), pages 125-26, 128-29 and 138-39.

1 Helen Wambach, *Life before Life* (New York: Bantam Books, 1979).

2 Hypnosis, even when done with the best of intentions, can make us spiritually vulnerable. It can open us to elements of the subconscious and unconscious of the practitioner. Through hypnosis we may also prematurely uncover records of events from past lives that we are not ready to deal with.

3 *Dharma* is Sanskrit for law. Dharma is the realization of the law of selfhood through adherence to cosmic law, including the laws of nature and a spiritual code of conduct such as the way or dharma of the Buddha

or the Christ. Dharma is one's duty to fulfill one's reason for being through the law of love and the sacred labor.

4 In an ectopic pregnancy the fertilized ovum develops outside the uterus (for instance, in the fallopian tubes) and the baby cannot live. The United States Department of Health and Human Services reported in 1984 that there has been a 300 percent increase in the United States in ectopic pregnancies since 1973— the year abortion was legalized. Researchers have also found that among women who have had one abortion, there is a 500 percent increase in ectopic pregnancies.

Additional Resources

The violet flame:

Elizabeth Clare Prophet, *Violet Flame to Heal Body, Mind and Soul* (Corwin Springs, Mont.: Summit University Press, 1997)

Elizabeth Clare Prophet, *The Creative Power of Sound: Affirmations to Create, Heal and Transform* (Summit University Press, 1998)

The spiritual life of the soul and the unborn:

Patricia Kirmond, *Messages from Heaven* (Summit University Press, 1999)

Elizabeth Clare Prophet, compiled and edited by Nancy Hearn and Dr. Joye Bennett, *Nurturing Your Baby's Soul: A Spiritual Guide for Expectant Parents* (Summit University Press, 1998)

For those facing the issue of abortion:

Free brochure: *What Women Need to Know About the Soul When Faced with Tough Decisions: Tough Choices About Pregnancy*
1-888-TheSoul
www.soulchoice.org

Further teachings of Elizabeth Clare Prophet on the subject of abortion:

Elizabeth Clare Prophet, *Life Begets Life,* audio recording A91060, available on CD-on-demand from:
www.SummitLighthouse.org/bookstore

For More Information

*F*or more information about The Summit Lighthouse Library, to place an order or to receive a free catalog of our books and products, please contact us at:

The Summit Lighthouse Library
PO Box 5000
Corwin Springs, MT 59030-5000
USA
Tel: 1-800-245-5445 or 406-848-9500
Fax: 1-800-221-8307 or 406-848-9555
www.tsl.org
tslinfo@tsl.org

*E*lizabeth Clare Prophet is a pioneer in modern spirituality and an internationally renowned author. For more than forty years she and her late husband, Mark Prophet, have published the teachings of the immortal saints and sages of East and West known as the ascended masters. Together they have given the world a new understanding of the ancient wisdom as well as a path of practical mysticism.

Neroli Duffy was trained as a medical doctor in Australia and England, and practiced in family medicine and anesthesia for ten years. As a woman physician she saw many patients who had personally faced the issue of abortion. Seeing first-hand the great need for healing of the soul, she now practices as a minister, writing and lecturing internationally on spirituality and healing and the teachings of the ascended masters. ✒

Acknowledgments

The concepts and ideas presented in this book are those of Elizabeth Clare Prophet. For over twenty years she has been giving a spiritual perspective on life in the womb. Many of the words are hers, and I take credit only for weaving the threads to make the whole.

Many people from all over the world have been touched by Mrs. Prophet's teachings on this subject. I hope that you, the reader, have also gained a new understanding of Life in all of its wonder.

NEROLI DUFFY